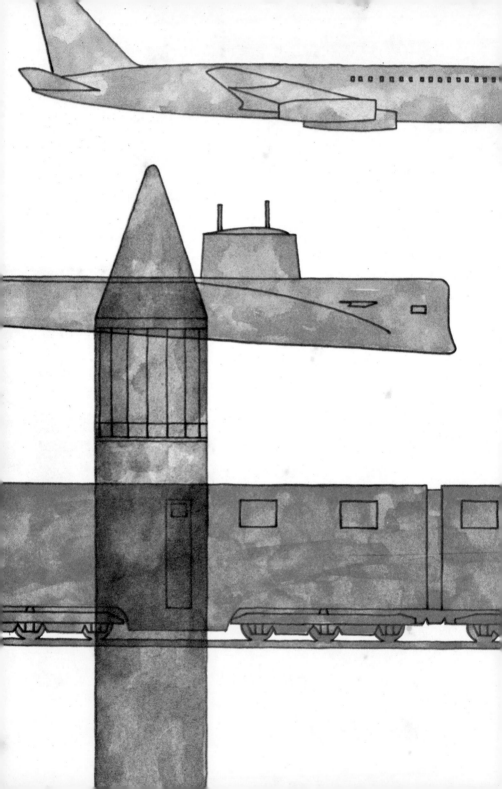

Engines

Progress and Power
by Don E. Rogers

illustrated by
George N. Roth

WHITMAN PUBLISHING COMPANY
RACINE, WISCONSIN

Photos appear through the courtesy of:

Allis-Chalmers Manufacturing Company: p. 48

Allison Division, General Motors Corporation: p. 54

General Motors Corporation: pp. 32, 36, 46

Jacobsen Manufacturing Company: pp. 44-45

Library of Congress Catalog Card Number: 62-13500

Printed in the U.S.A. by
Western Printing and Lithographing Company

Contents

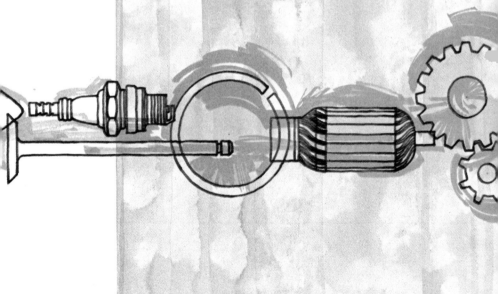

MAN, MUSCLE, AND ROCKETS

TODAY WE LIVE IN AN AGE OF POWER— power produced by engines. The thundering roar of a great jet airliner as it hurtles down the runway is the sound of engine power. The buzzing of a doorbell and the whirring of a power lawn mower are also the sounds of engine power. Engines are an important part of our daily lives. But this was not always the case.

The human body might be called the first engine. In the beginning man used his own muscles to travel great distances and to lift and carry things. Almost four thousand years before the birth of Christ, the great pyramid of Cheops in Egypt was built by the muscles of men. This great tomb is 425 feet high. It is made of huge stone blocks, each weighing as much as sixty tons. To build it, the muscles of a hundred thousand slaves were used— slaves working for twenty years.

Sometime later, man learned to use the muscles of animals. The ox was tamed and made to pull a plow. Camels, elephants, and mules were used for carrying loads or riders. The horse was found to be the best for carrying man on its back.

No one is exactly sure when man first began to use the energy of the wind and the water to do his work. A cave man perhaps discovered that the current of a flowing river would carry a raft downstream. The first Egyptian sailboats would go only in the direction of the wind. Much later the Norsemen learned how to rig a sail so their boats would also go against the wind.

About two thousand years ago in the country that is now Italy a Roman built the first water wheel. The swift-flowing current of the Tiber River was used to turn a large paddle wheel. The paddle-wheel shaft, with the aid of two gears, was used to drive a millstone for grinding grain. This ancient wheel was probably the first real "engine" built by man.

The Roman water wheel and the Egyptian sailboat are the ancestors of modern engines. Today steam turbines produce electricity. Diesel engines power great ships. Turbojet engines thrust supersonic airplanes through the skies. And one day soon, rocket engines will carry man into space. The how and why of these engines is the story of this book.

NATURE HOLDS THE ENERGY

THE STORY OF ENGINES is the story of energy, work, and power. In talking about engines the words *energy, work,* and *power* have very important meanings.

In order to move something a force must be exerted by pushing or pulling. Work is done whenever a force moves something through a distance. Work is done when the wind blows, because air is moving. Work is done when a river flows, because water is moving. Anything which has the ability to do work is *energy.*

Even a motionless object can have energy, just because of its position. A stone resting at the top of a hill can be moved so that it will roll down and do work. Its position gives it energy.

This rock has potential energy. Its position makes it able to do work if it is pushed.

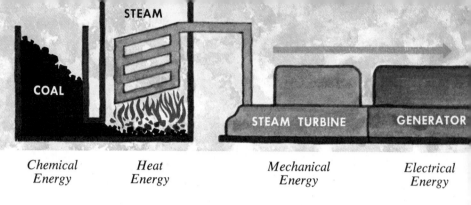

| Chemical Energy | Heat Energy | Mechanical Energy | Electrical Energy |

Energy Can Be Changed From One Form to Another

In the world we live in there are many kinds of energy. Deep in a quarry a dynamite explosion throws great rocks about like pebbles. The chemical energy in the dynamite has broken and thrown the rocks.

The snarl of a power saw slicing through a piece of wood is the sound of mechanical energy. But the whirling saw blade is turned by an electric motor. Therefore electricity must also be a form of energy.

The amazing thing about energy is that it may be changed from one kind to another. Think about burning a piece of coal. Burning takes place when the carbon in the coal and the oxygen in the air combine chemically. When this happens heat energy is given off. Chemical energy has then changed into heat energy.

The heat given off by the burning coal can be used to boil water. This makes steam. The steam can be made to run a steam engine. In this case the heat energy is turned into mechanical energy by the steam engine.

12

When coal is burned the chemical energy in the coal is changed to heat energy. If the heat is used to boil water, steam is produced. Then the heat energy can be converted to mechanical energy by a steam turbine . . . the mechanical energy to electrical energy by a generator . . . and the electrical energy can be changed to chemical energy by a storage battery or back to heat energy by an iron.

Now suppose the steam engine runs a generator which makes electricity. The mechanical energy of the steam engine would then be used to produce electrical energy.

The electrical energy from the generator could be used to charge a storage battery. We would then be changing electrical energy back into chemical energy. We might also use the electricity to heat an electric iron. Then we would be changing electrical energy back into heat energy.

The sun is the source of all of our energy. The sun's heat energy sets warm air moving. This produces the winds which drive windmills. The sun's heat causes water to evaporate from puddles, lakes, and oceans. It is this

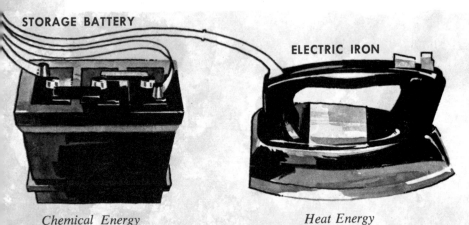

STORAGE BATTERY

ELECTRIC IRON

Chemical Energy

Heat Energy

water falling to the earth from the clouds which produces our swift-running streams and rivers. The chemical energy in coal comes from sunlight which shone on the earth millions of years ago.

What does it mean then when we talk about the power of an engine? To understand power we must think about how fast work is done.

Horsepower

The first steam engines were built to pump water out of coal mines. It was natural to compare the work which an engine could do to the amount of work done by the horses. This is the reason that the power of engines today is measured in *horsepower*.

One horsepower is the ability to lift 33,000 pounds one foot in one minute. Horsepower measures the speed at which an engine can do work. If you weigh one hundred

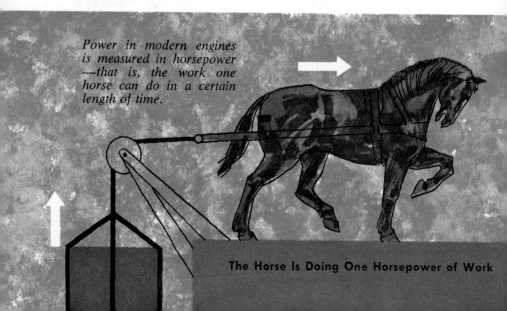

Power in modern engines is measured in horsepower —that is, the work one horse can do in a certain length of time.

The Horse Is Doing One Horsepower of Work

A child running upstairs puts out from one-eighth to one-tenth horse-power. Three-quarters of the way through a hundred yard dash an Olympic sprinter could, for a fleeting instant, put out as much as eight horsepower. He would average about four horsepower for the entire race.

pounds and walk up a flight of stairs ten feet high, you do one thousand foot-pounds of work. But the amount of horsepower you use will depend upon the time it takes you to climb the stairs. It takes more power to lift a load quickly than to lift the same load slowly. We can see then that the power of an engine is determined not only by the work it puts out, but also by how fast it does this work.

The horses used in the old coal mines must have been very strong and well trained. Modern horses do not generally produce as much as 33,000 foot-pounds in one minute. A *manpower* is usually estimated at about one-tenth of one horsepower, but only for a short time.

Efficiency Counts, Too

Another important idea in connection with engines is efficiency. The job of an engine is to get as much work as possible out of the energy with which it is supplied. The efficiency of an engine tells us how much of the energy is turned into useful work.

In a steam locomotive only about 5 per cent of the energy in the coal is changed into useful work. The great steam turbines which generate electricity are more efficient. About 20 per cent of the energy in the coal is changed to electrical energy. The big diesels which power huge trucks use their fuel even more efficiently. Almost 50 per cent of the energy in the fuel is changed into work. The huge water turbines which generate electricity at great dams are among the most efficient engines of all. More than 90 per cent of the energy in the flowing water is changed to electrical energy for lighting cities.

The sun shining, the wind blowing, water moving, coal and oil burning, electricity flowing—all of these forms of energy and many more work for man, but only when they are controlled by the wonderful engines man designs.

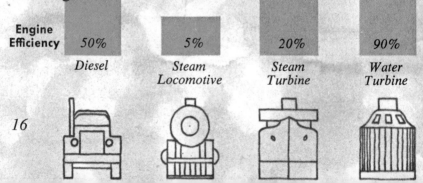

Engine Efficiency	50%	5%	20%	90%
	Diesel	Steam Locomotive	Steam Turbine	Water Turbine

16

POWER FROM WATER-TURNED WHEELS

LIFT A PAIL OF WATER. The downward pull you feel on your arm is the pull of gravity. It is this gravitational force or weight which turned the early overshot water wheel.

This water wheel had a number of buckets around the rim. A trough called a flume carried the water to the top of the wheel. The weight of the water in the buckets on one side of the wheel made it turn. The water spilled out of the downward-moving buckets near the bottom of the wheel. The empty, lighter buckets then rose up the other side of the wheel to be filled again at the top.

Where there was no natural waterfall, the stream was dammed to raise the level of the water so the overshot water wheel could operate. A kind of sliding door called a gate valve was moved up and down in the flume to control the flow of water to the wheel.

The Overshot Water Wheel

Buckets catch the water and spill it. The fallen water, its energy removed, is called tail water.

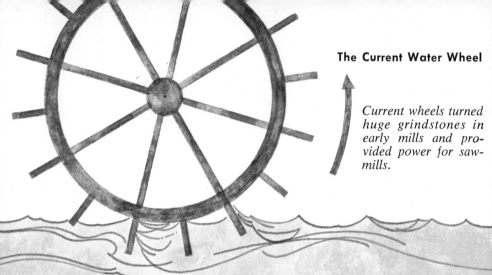

The Current Water Wheel

Current wheels turned huge grindstones in early mills and provided power for sawmills.

Other early water wheels were built along swiftly moving streams. These were called current wheels or undershot water wheels.

Flowing water possesses kinetic energy, that is, energy which produces force by striking or collision. The more the energy, the greater the force will be. Anything that is moving has this kind of energy. The force produced by kinetic energy is felt when you hold your hand in front of a garden hose. It is this force which pushes your hand away when the water strikes it. And it is this force, kinetic energy, which turned the early current wheels.

These large water wheels had paddles around the edge which dipped into the stream. The moving water struck the blades and turned the wheel. It was found that anything which would make the water flow faster would make the wheel run better. This was because faster flowing water has more energy. It could hit the paddles harder.

18

These wheels were not very efficient. They were used only where water at high levels was not available.

Better Than the Water Wheel

Modern water turbines are much more efficient and powerful than the ancient wheels, even though some still make use of kinetic energy. The Pelton turbine is a wheel, generally made of steel, with many cuplike blades mounted about its rim. Water moving at a very high speed strikes against the bottom blades. This causes the wheel to turn rapidly. Nozzles are used to speed up the water and aim it at the blades.

The high-speed water jet used to turn the wheel comes from the energy caused by the pressure of water at a great height. The weight of water in a tall pipe exerts a great force on the nozzles at the bottom. This weight or pressure forces the water to speed up through the nozzles.

The distance water falls from the dam to the nozzle is called its head. The greater the head, the faster the water jet travels out of the nozzle.

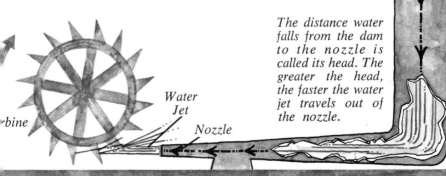

Water Jet

Nozzle

bine

The Pelton Turbine

Reaction turbines are always completely under water. The used water flows out through a pipe at the bottom of the turbine. The turbine wheel shaft extends through another chamber to drive an electric generator.

Still More Improvements

Other kinds of modern water turbines depend upon what is called a reaction force. It is reaction force which makes a garden hose push back against your hand when you hold it. Have you ever dropped a running garden hose? It is the backward reaction force which makes the hose twist and wiggle about on the ground. Anything which produces a jet—a rush of gas or liquid—experiences this same reaction force. Some modern water turbines are built to use this force of reaction.

In a reaction turbine the moving blades act like nozzles and speed up the water. The Francis turbine has a large outer case with a number of blades to direct the water into the inner moving wheel. The water enters at the sides of this outer speed ring and flows through to strike the blades on the inside runner. As the water passes between the blades of the inside runner it speeds up. The reaction force of the water turns the blades of the runner at high speed.

20

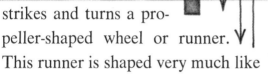

The Propeller Turbine

Here the force of falling water is changed to mechanical energy. This in turn is changed to electrical energy.

The propeller turbine is another kind of turbine. Here the water strikes and turns a propeller-shaped wheel or runner. This runner is shaped very much like the propeller of a great ship. It works like a ship's propeller in reverse. Instead of the propeller driving the water, the moving water drives the propeller.

Creating Water Power

The amount of "head"—the distance the water falls—determines which of these turbines will work best. When the head is sixty feet or less, the propeller turbine is best. The Francis reaction turbine is most often used with heads between sixty and eight hundred feet. These types are used where the water speed cannot be made very high. The Pelton water wheel, however, depends upon great water jet speed. It is built where the fall of the water is anywhere from one thousand feet to as much as 2500 feet. In a plant in Switzerland the water actually falls 5700 feet and travels three hundred feet per second as it hits the blades!

A generating station where electricity is generated by water power is called a hydroelectric plant. Modern water turbines are used almost completely for turning electric generators. As the water rushes into the huge turbines that are connected to the generators the energy in the moving water is changed into electrical energy.

Artificial lakes and dams are built to store water and increase its head. The water at a high level in the dam is carried to the turbines through great pipes called penstocks. The head of the water produces a great pressure at the nozzle end. The penstock pipes must be very strong. The water flowing to the turbine is controlled by a gate valve at the bottom of the penstock.

A water turbine develops great power in a small space. One large turbine at Niagara Falls develops seventy thousand horsepower. It uses only a small amount of water which would otherwise flow unused over the Falls.

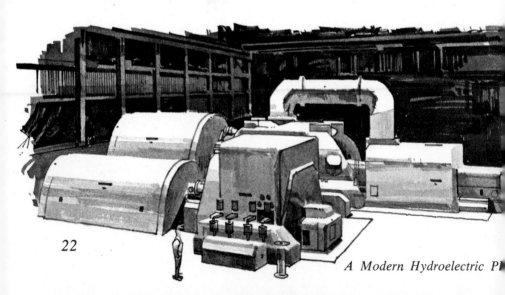

A Modern Hydroelectric P

HEAT+STEAM=POWER

MEN HAD BURNED WOOD AND COAL for thousands of years—but only for cooking, warmth, and light. The steam engine was the first machine to use the energy of heat for lifting and turning.

Steam is formed by the heating and boiling of water. Steam is water changed to a hot invisible gas. This gas takes up more space than the water did. As steam cools, it condenses, changing back into tiny drops of water that again take up less space. If used correctly, steam has great forces for pushing and pulling. Its pushing power makes the lid of a pan dance up and down when water is boiled.

More than two thousand years ago Hero of Alexandria used the heat energy in steam to spin a ball about rapidly. Hero's spinning ball was the first steam turbine.

The first steam engine was this invention of Hero of Alexandria. Fire heated water in an enclosed tub. Steam escaped by passing up through pipes into the ball and out through two angled nozzles. This caused the ball to revolve because the steam was being forced out in opposite directions.

It was just a toy, however, and not a useful engine. Seventeen hundred years passed before men were able to use the energy in steam.

In 1705 Thomas Newcomen, an English blacksmith, built the first steam engine to pump water out of coal mines. Newcomen's engine was slow and noisy. It made only six to eight pumping strokes in a minute. It was, however, better than men and horses. By 1767 there were sixty Newcomen engines in use in the mines.

Newcomen's engine used the energy of steam to move a piston. A metal cylinder, open at one end, held the piston. Steam was let in at the bottom of the cylinder, under the piston. The pushing power of the steam forced the piston up.

When the piston reached the top of its stroke, water was squirted into the cylinder. This condensed the steam. As the steam condensed,

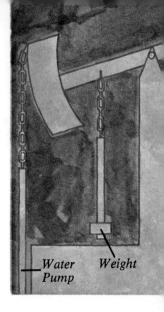

Water Pump   Weight

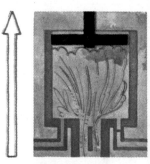

1. Steam is let in.

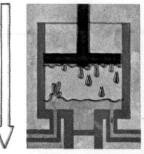

2. Water is squirted in, condensing the steam.

Cylinder, Open at the Top

Boiler

'ire

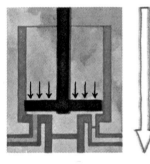

3. *Outside air pressure forces piston down.*

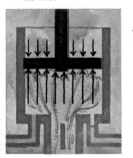

4. *Steam is let in again.*

it took up less space and so produced a low pressure or vacuum. The outside air pressure on the top of the piston—now greater than the pressure under the piston—then forced it back down.

The Newcomen engine was not efficient. It used great amounts of coal and was expensive to run. It was a Scotch mechanic, James Watt, who discovered the real secret of steam power.

The Real Thing

The Watt engine had two great improvements. The steam was not cooled and condensed under the piston. Instead it flowed into a tank where it turned to water. This kept the power cylinder from cooling off between strokes. Fuel was not wasted heating up the cylinder again each time.

Piston Movements of the Newcomen Engine

Repeated heating and cooling made the piston move up and down in the cylinder. The piston rod carried the force to a water pump.

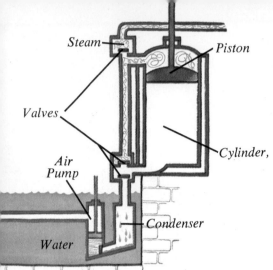

Steam

Piston

Valves

Air
Pump

Cylinder,

Condenser

Water

Watt's Engine

Watt's engine produced three times more power from each pound of coal than had the Newcomen engine.

Also this cylinder was closed at the top, instead of being open as in the New-comen engine. Steam was let into the cylinder on each side of the piston by valves. The steam pushed the piston both ways, speeding up the action of the engine and delivering more power.

The reciprocating or back-and-forth steam engine was widely used about fifty years ago. It powered generators, factory machinery, sawmills, air pumps, and even pile drivers. This engine is the father of our present internal combustion engines.

This Is How It Works

A steam engine has two main parts, a boiler and an engine. The boiler is a water tank in which steam is produced by the heat from burning fuel. Steam from the boiler passes through a pipe to the engine. The engine changes the heat energy in the steam into mechanical energy to do work.

The reciprocating steam engine has a cylinder, piston,

and valves to control the steam flow. The piston fits the cylinder closely, but moves easily back and forth. A piston rod is attached to the piston and moves with it. It pushes or pulls upon the connecting rod. The connecting rod connects to a crank on the engine shaft. The crank changes the back-and-forth movement of the piston into a turning motion of the engine shaft.

A slide valve lets the steam into and out of the cylinder. This valve is moved back and forth by the valve rod and this is, in turn, moved by the engine shaft. As the slide valve moves, it opens and closes the cylinder ports or openings.

Steam passes through inlet ports at one end of the cylinder, filling the cylinder. The pressure of the steam pushes against the piston, moving it to the other end. The piston, the piston rod, the connecting rod and the crank are all attached. They move together, turning the engine shaft. At the end of the piston stroke, a flywheel

The Steam Engine

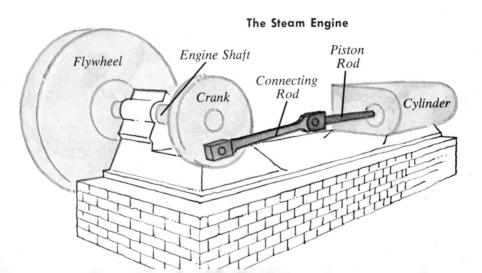

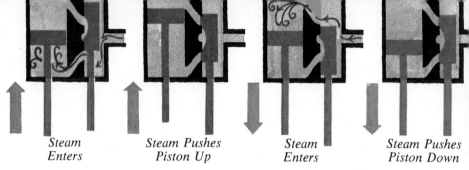

Steam Enters | Steam Pushes Piston Up | Steam Enters | Steam Pushes Piston Down

Piston Movements in a Reciprocating Steam Engine

continues to turn the crankshaft. The piston then moves back in the opposite direction.

At the same time the valve rod moves the slide valve, closing the inlet port and opening the exhaust port. The used steam rushes out of the cylinder. On the piston's return trip, the slide valve admits steam to the opposite end of the cylinder. The pressure of the new steam pushes the piston back in the opposite direction.

These actions happen over and over again and are called a cycle. The flywheel keeps the engine moving smoothly through the cycle.

And Then, Something New

In the year 1867 a small ship called the *Turbinia* appeared off the coast of England. This amazing vessel raced through the water leaving all other ships far behind. The secret of her speed was a new kind of engine called a steam turbine.

A steam turbine has no cylinders or pistons. It uses the energy of expanding steam to push against the blades of a turbine wheel. The steam turbine, like the Pelton water turbine, is turned by the striking force of a high-speed jet.

A steam jet however travels much faster than a water jet. Because of this, a steam turbine wheel turns at very high speeds. It is not unusual for small steam turbines to spin at thirty thousand turns per minute or five hundred in one second.

The first turbines had only one wheel turning the drive shaft. Later inventors added a number of turbine wheels to one shaft. In this way the energy in the steam could be put to work in small stages, one after the other.

Modern steam turbines have several wheels on one shaft. Each wheel has a great many curved blades around its rim. Each of the revolving wheels is separated by a ring of fixed blades. The turning wheels are called rotors. The rows of fixed blades are called stators because they do not move.

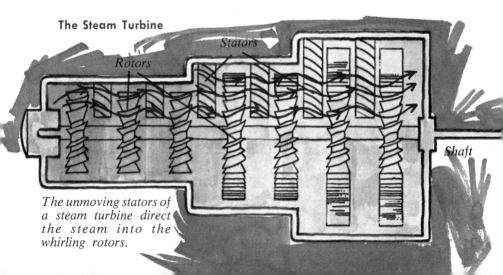

The Steam Turbine

Stators

Rotors

Shaft

The unmoving stators of a steam turbine direct the steam into the whirling rotors.

The pressure energy of the hot steam from the boiler is changed into a high speed jet by tapered nozzles. These nozzles direct the steam against the blades of the first wheel. The blast of steam striking the curved blades of the rotor forces it to turn.

The fixed stator blades aim the moving steam. Each row of stator blades turns the steam in the right direction to strike the blades of the next whirling rotor. As the steam passes through the rows of rotors and stators it loses both pressure and speed. The heat energy in the steam has been changed to the mechanical energy of the whirling rotors. Thus the steam energy is used as it weaves its way through the many sets of blades in the turbine.

In a modern power plant hot steam is speeded up by the nozzles to twelve hundred miles per hour. The steam jet striking the blades is twelve times faster than a hurricane. In an average turbine the steam passes through from seventeen to twenty wheels and pushes against five thousand blades. The very high rotating speed makes it particularly useful for driving electric generators.

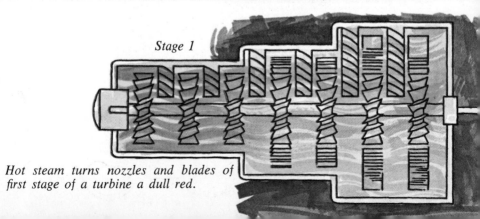

Stage 1

Hot steam turns nozzles and blades of first stage of a turbine a dull red.

INTERNAL COMBUSTION...
OPENS THE WAY

THE MOST IMPORTANT OF THE heat engines is the internal combustion engine. There is really no other source of power which can replace it.

The big difference between the steam power plant and the internal combustion engine is where the combustion or burning takes place. In the steam power plant, the fuel is burned under a boiler away from the engine or turbine. *Internal combustion* means *inside burning*—fuel is burned inside the engine itself. However, the power in either engine is still produced by a piston moving back and forth inside a cylinder.

The fuel used in an internal combustion engine is usually oil or gasoline. By themselves these cannot give power. They must be mixed with air to burn. For this reason the internal combustion engine is sometimes called an air-breathing engine.

The oxygen in the air is the key which unlocks the stored chemical energy in the gasoline. This great energy comes from the sun shining millions of years ago.

1898 De Dion
Bouton

Nitroglycerin and dyna-
mite are thought of as
being powerful. Gasoline
however has six times as
much energy as nitroglycerin
and eight times the energy of
dynamite!

The Gasoline Engine

The gasoline engine operates on a cycle. This means
that just like the steam engine it runs by doing a certain
number of things over and over again. The gasoline
engine is also called an Otto cycle engine. This is in honor
of its German inventor, Dr. N. A. Otto, who first built
and ran one almost one hundred years ago.

The heart of this engine is the familiar piston and
cylinder combination. Inside the cylinder a closely fitting
piston slides smoothly up and down. The cylinder is
closed at one end to form the combustion chamber. The
cylinder has two valves to allow gasoline and air to enter
and leave the closed chamber.

The piston is joined to a connecting rod by a wrist pin.
The wrist pin acts as a hinge for the connecting rod. The

32

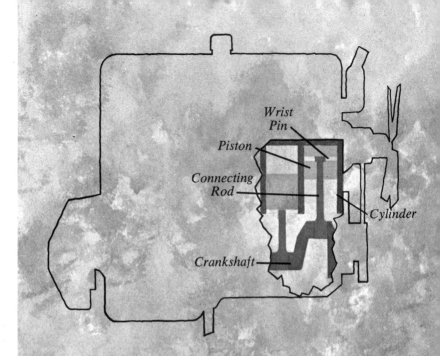

Wrist Pin

Piston

Connecting Rod

Cylinder

Crankshaft

other end of the connecting rod is joined to the crank which is part of the engine crankshaft.

When the piston moves, the wrist pin makes the connecting rod move also. Since the connecting rod is joined to the crankshaft, the crankshaft must also move. But the crankshaft can only spin around in a circular fashion. The back-and-forth motion of the piston therefore causes a turning motion of the engine crankshaft. It is the spinning crankshaft which turns the wheels of a car or the propeller of an airplane.

This Is How It Works

The best way to understand how a gasoline engine operates is to follow a complete cycle. The first part of

33

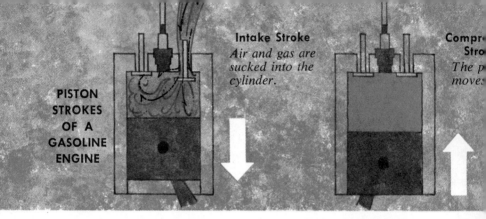

Intake Stroke
Air and gas are sucked into the cylinder.

**Compr...
Stro...**
The p... move:

It is really the chemical energy in the fuel which pushes down the piston, turning the crankshaft. The mixture must burn rapidly but not explode. An exploding mixture would move the piston with a blow. A steadily burning mixture moves the piston in a series of smooth pushes.

the cycle happens as the piston moves from the top to the bottom of the cylinder. It is called the *intake stroke*. During this stroke the intake valve is open. The downward movement of the piston sucks a charge of air and gasoline into the cylinder.

When the piston starts to move from bottom to top, both valves are closed. Since the mixture of gasoline and air cannot escape, it is squeezed together, compressed. When this happens, the mixture struggles violently to escape. This is called a *compression stroke* because it raises the pressure of the mixture.

When the piston reaches the top of the cylinder an electric spark starts the compressed mixture burning. The hot gases formed by the combustion push the piston down like a powerful hand. This downward movement of the piston is called the *power stroke*.

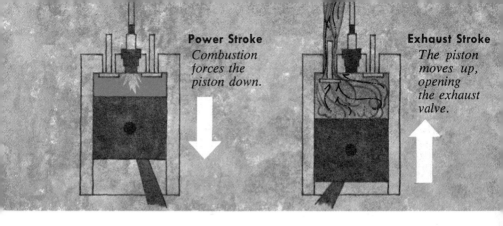

Power Stroke
*Combustion
forces the
piston down.*

Exhaust Stroke
*The piston
moves up,
opening
the exhaust
valve.*

When the piston is at the end of the power stroke, the space above it is filled with expanded, burned gas. Before the engine can take in a fresh charge, the old one must be removed. The last stroke then is the *exhaust stroke.* As the piston moves up in the cylinder the exhaust valve opens. The moving piston forces the burned gas out into the exhaust pipe.

The crankshaft turns twice to complete a cycle. Each cycle is made up of four strokes of the piston: intake, compression, power, and exhaust. This is sometimes called a four-stroke cycle engine. Only one stroke of the four helps to turn the crankshaft. The rest of the time, the crankshaft is making the piston go up and down.

Flywheels, Valves, and Camshafts

Every engine has a flywheel. It is this heavy wheel attached to the crankshaft which keeps it turning smoothly. Modern engines have four, six, eight, or even more cylinders turning the same crankshaft. This makes a more powerful engine and the cylinders can help each other. In an in-line engine they are lined up one behind the other. The crankshaft is built so that there is always a power stroke happening in one of the cylinders. This makes the job of the flywheel much easier.

Sometimes the cylinders are in two rows. They are set at an angle and drive the same crankshaft. When there are eight cylinders this is called a V-8 engine.

The cylinders are all put together in one block of metal called the cylinder block. The top of the cylinders is covered by another part called the cylinder head. The cylinder head has holes for spark plugs and sometimes for valves. The crankcase holds the crankshaft in place and covers the whirling cranks.

Each cylinder must have two valves: one for intake

The V-8 Engine

1. *Crankshaft*
2. *Connecting Rod*
3. *Piston and Wrist Pin*
4. *Exhaust Valve*
5. *Spark Plug*
6. *Camshaft*
7. *Carburetor*
8. *Cylinder Wall*
9. *Cooling Water Jacket*
10. *Crankcase*

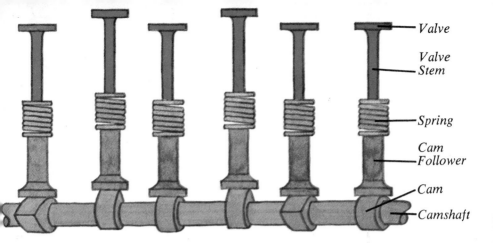

Valve
Valve Stem
Spring
Cam Follower
Cam
Camshaft

The camshaft opens and closes the intake and exhaust valves of each cylinder. As the camshaft rotates, each valve is in turn forced open with precision timing.

and one for exhaust. Each valve must open and close at just the right time in the cycle. This must be done very quickly—in less than 1/100 of a second! This difficult job is done by a very important part of the engine called the camshaft.

The camshaft has a number of egg-shaped bumps on it called cams. There are two cams for every engine cylinder: one for the exhaust valve and one for the intake valve. A six-cylinder engine would have twelve cams on its camshaft. It is the bumpy shape of the cam which opens the valve as the camshaft is turned.

Each valve stem sits on a cam follower which follows the up-and-down motion of the cam. The upward motion of the cam opens the valve. When the cam turns downward a strong spring pulls the valve down, closing it. A crankshaft changes up-and-down motion to turning motion; a camshaft changes a turning motion to an up-and-down motion.

The camshaft is turned by the crankshaft. It is connected to the crankshaft by gears at the end of the engine opposite the flywheel. The camshaft gear is just twice as big as the crankshaft gear. This makes each valve open only once during two turns of the crankshaft. The camshaft must be made with the cams in exactly the right places and be connected correctly to the crankshaft. If it is not, the valves will not open and close at the right time —and the engine will not run.

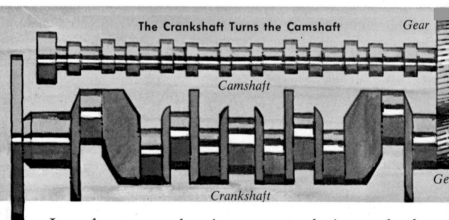

The Crankshaft Turns the Camshaft *Gear*

Camshaft

Ge

Crankshaft

In order to complete its power-producing cycle the internal combustion engine needs air, fuel, and electricity. The carburetor, the valves, and the spark plugs all work together to keep the crankshaft spinning..

PISTON ENGINES SERVE TODAY'S NEEDS...

MODERN AUTOMOBILE ENGINES must be fed air and gasoline very carefully. For smooth and efficient burning these must be mixed in just the right amounts. Engineers have found that each pound of gasoline should be mixed with about fifteen pounds of air.

In automobiles the gasoline is pumped from the gas tank up to the carburetor. The carburetor does two things. It breaks up the gasoline into tiny drops. It also mixes the right amount of gasoline with the incoming air.

The carburetor works much like a paint spray gun. Air, sucked in by the engine cylinders, rushes through a tube which is narrow at the center. In the narrow part of the tube the air passes over a small nozzle which supplies a spray of gasoline. The fast-moving air picks up tiny droplets of gasoline and mixes with them. Thus the mixture

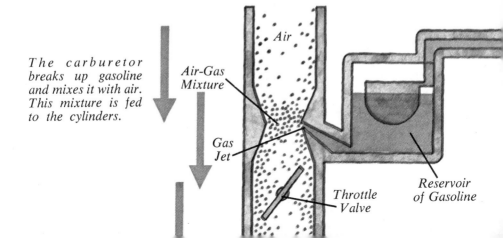

The carburetor breaks up gasoline and mixes it with air. This mixture is fed to the cylinders.

Air

Air-Gas Mixture

Gas Jet

Throttle Valve

Reservoir of Gasoline

fed to the engine cylinders is a mist of air and gasoline.

The carburetor throttle valve works much like the damper in a stovepipe. It controls the amount of air and gasoline going to the cylinders. In an automobile, the throttle valve is connected to the accelerator pedal.

Pushing down the pedal opens the throttle valve. As it opens, more of the gasoline-air mixture is fed to the cylinders. This makes the engine turn faster and deliver more power. More power to the wheels makes the car go faster.

Spark Plugs, Generators, and Cooling

All gasoline engines must have some way of burning the gasoline-air mixture. A spark plug or sometimes two fit tightly into the wall of the combustion chamber. A spark jumps across a narrow gap between two wires at the end of the spark plug. This spark starts the gasoline-air mixture burning.

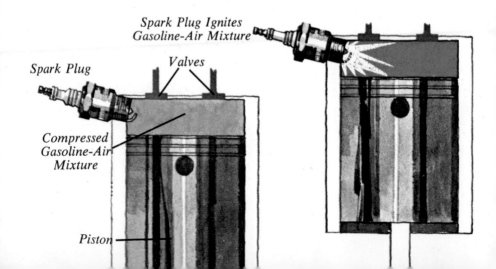

Spark Plug Ignites
Gasoline-Air Mixture

Spark Plug

Valves

Compressed
Gasoline-Air
Mixture

Piston

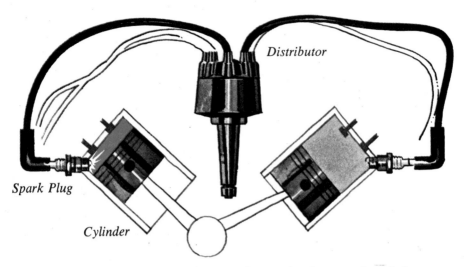

Distributor

Spark Plug

Cylinder

Electrical energy is led to each spark plug at the right time by wires connected to the distributor. This is a spinning switch with one arm like a clock hand. Since it must work with the valves and piston it is also turned by the crankshaft. As it spins, electricity is sent out to each spark plug at just the right time. A six-cylinder engine driving a car at eighty miles per hour has to have twelve thousand separate sparks in a minute!

The electricity for the spark plugs comes from a small electrical generator. The generator is driven by the engine. Some of the power produced by the engine is used, then, to keep the engine running.

Engines must also be kept cool. The burned gases in the cylinders are hot enough to melt the metal of the engine. To prevent this, water is pumped through the cylinder block. The same water is used over and over again. When it becomes hot it is pumped to a radiator and cooled by air. A fan, driven by the engine, draws air around the cooling tubes of the radiator. After passing through the cooling tubes the water flows back through the engine again.

To cool an engine water is passed over it in a continuous cycle.

Friction can also destroy an engine. Two pieces of metal rubbing against each other become hot due to friction. Friction wears away metal parts very quickly. Fortunately a thin film of oil between rubbing surfaces will greatly reduce wear. This is why all moving metal parts in an engine must be kept covered with oil.

Designers of engines are always looking for new ways to make them smaller, lighter, and more powerful. The four-stroke cycle engine bothered engineers because it required two turns of the crankshaft to get one power-producing stroke of the piston. It was this line of thinking which produced the two-stroke cycle engine.

The Two-Stroke Cycle Engine

This engine accomplishes the tasks of intake, compression, power, and exhaust in two strokes of the piston.

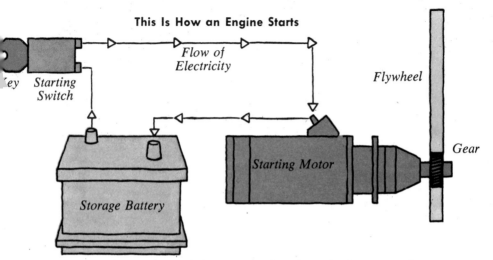

This Is How an Engine Starts

Flow of Electricity

'ey   Starting Switch

Flywheel

Gear

Starting Motor

Storage Battery

A starting switch causes stored electricity to flow from the battery to the starting motor. The starting motor turns a gear on the flywheel and makes it revolve. The flywheel makes all the moving parts of the engine operate. The engine then creates electricity, which is in turn stored in the storage battery.

It delivers one power stroke for each turn of the crankshaft. Because of this, a two-stroke cycle engine will give more power than a four-stroke cycle engine of the same size and weight.

A two-cycle engine has pistons, connecting rods, and a crankshaft, much like its four-cycle cousin. In addition to its usual job however the piston now takes the place of the valves. The crankcase of a two-cycle engine also does double duty. It must be made as small as possible and be gas-tight. It not only covers the whirling crankshaft but is filled with the gas-air mixture from the carburetor.

The power stroke starts as the gasoline-air mixture is ignited by an electric spark. On the downward power

43

stroke the piston compresses the gasoline-air mixture in the crankcase. Near the bottom of the stroke the exhaust port is opened and the burned gases rush out. At the very bottom of the power stroke the piston uncovers the transfer port. This is across the cylinder from the exhaust port. It connects the crankcase to the combustion chamber. A new partly compressed charge flows from the crankcase through the transfer port into the cylinder.

As the piston rises upward it closes both the transfer port and the exhaust port. The new charge trapped in the cylinder is compressed by the rising piston. When the piston is at the top of its stroke, the vacuum in the

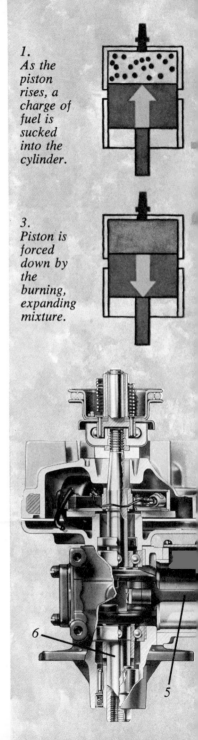

1.
As the piston rises, a charge of fuel is sucked into the cylinder.

3.
Piston is forced down by the burning, expanding mixture.

6

5

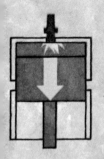

2.
Gasoline-air mixture is ignited by the spark.

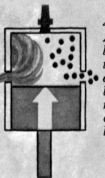

4.
At the bottom of the stroke exhaust is let out, a new charge let in.

A small two-cycle engine like his powers a lawn mower.

1. Spark Plug
2. Combustion Chamber
3. Piston
4. Exhaust Port
5. Connecting Rod
6. Crankshaft
7. Cooling Fins

crankcase sucks in a new charge from the carburetor. The spark plug ignites the mixture and the cycle starts again.

The two-cycle engine is simpler and less expensive than other engines because it does not have a camshaft or valves. But because both the exhaust port and the transfer port are open at the same time some fuel is always wasted. Some of the new charge is swept out with the old and some of the burned gas stays behind in the cylinder. Because of this it requires more fuel and is not very efficient. Two-cycle engines are ideal where small size, small weight, and low power are needed. They are used for power lawn mowers and motorboats.

45

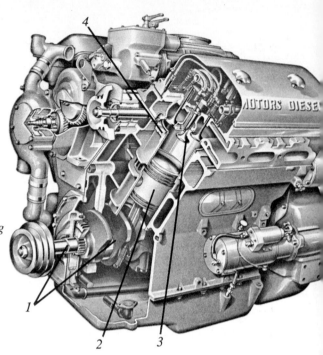

Diesel engines are used where great power is needed—in trucks, trains, and in heavy machinery. They have even been used in submarines.

1. *Crankshaft, Including Balancing Weights*
2. *Piston*
3. *Valves*
4. *Cylinder Wall Liner*

The Big Diesels

Where great power and high efficiency are needed, such as for powering trains and trucks, nothing can beat the diesel engine. About 1892 its inventor, Dr. Rudolph Diesel, built his first engine. It exploded and almost killed him. Five years later however the first successful diesel engine was built.

The diesel engine is based on the fact that air becomes warmer as it is compressed or squeezed down. With enough compression, the air can be made to ignite the fuel. This is why a diesel engine does not need spark plugs. To keep the burning from starting too soon, only

46

air is compressed in the cylinder. A special pump called an injector shoots fuel into the cylinder at just the right moment for combustion.

The four-cycle diesel works very much like the Otto cycle engine. On the intake stroke only air is drawn into the cylinder. The compression stroke squeezes the air into a small space in the top of the cylinder. A mist of fuel oil is then sprayed into the cylinder. The air is so hot that the fuel ignites and burns immediately. The hot gases expand and force the piston down on the power stroke.

The exhaust stroke completes the cycle with the piston forcing the burned gases out the exhaust valve. It is now ready for the next cycle.

The pistons, crankshaft, and connecting rods of the diesel are much heavier and stronger than those in the gasoline engine. This is because of the great compression pressures in the diesel engine. A diesel must also be oiled and cooled just as an automobile engine is.

The fuel injector measures the exact amount of fuel

Piston Strokes of a Four-Cycle Diesel Engine

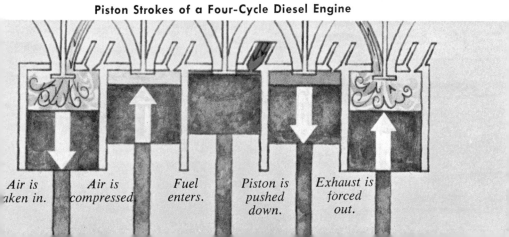

| Air is taken in. | Air is compressed. | Fuel enters. | Piston is pushed down. | Exhaust is forced out. |

for each injection. The speed of a diesel engine is controlled by changing the amount of fuel injected. The injector on a diesel-powered truck makes six thousand separate injections in a mile. It divides one gallon of diesel oil into 120,000 parts.

Early diesel engines ran at very slow speeds and were very heavy. Many years passed before they were made small enough and light enough for use in trucks and trains. Diesel engines are now built in many sizes both large and small. The modern high-speed diesels power boats, tractors, trucks, buses, and even oil-well machinery.

1. Diesel Engine
2. Radiator
3. Valves
4. Cylinder
5. Piston
6. Crankshaft
7. Crankcase
8. Drive Clutch
9. Power Transmission
10. Steering Clutch
11. Fuel Tank
12. Oil Bath Air Cleaner

POWER FOR FLIGHT

MAN'S CONQUEST OF THE AIR would not have been possible without the invention of the internal combustion engine. It was the only engine which could be made small and light, yet powerful enough to thrust an airplane into the skies.

The crankshaft of an airplane engine is used to turn a propeller. It is the spinning propeller which produces the powerful thrust which pushes the airplane forward. It works much like the propeller of a ship. The spinning blades are shaped to catch the air and throw it backward. In being thrown back by the blades, the air produces a reaction force, a thrust, on the propeller. It is this reaction force which pushes the airplane forward.

Turning a propeller requires power. This power comes from the spinning crankshaft of the engine. Aircraft

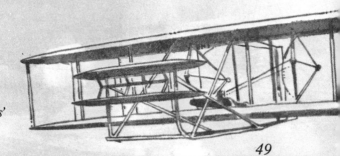

The Wright Brothers' Plane, the Flyer

engines operate on the same idea as the automobile engine, but they are much lighter. An automobile engine of the same power as an aircraft engine would be about ten times heavier.

Airplane engines are made in many sizes and shapes. Some engines have the cylinders in a V shape. Others have them directly behind each other. One of the most interesting kinds is the radial engine. In this the cylinders radiate from the crankcase like the spokes of a wheel from its hub.

Like all internal combustion engines, aircraft engines must be cooled. They may be either air-cooled or liquid-cooled. The air-cooled type have a great many thin fins on the cylinders. The air blast from the propeller blows over the fins, cooling the engine. In liquid-cooled engines a liquid is pumped through cooling jackets to carry away the heat. For this kind of engine a radiator is needed.

Few people know that propeller-driven planes cannot fly much faster than four hundred miles an hour. Why? At speeds of much more than four hundred miles an hour

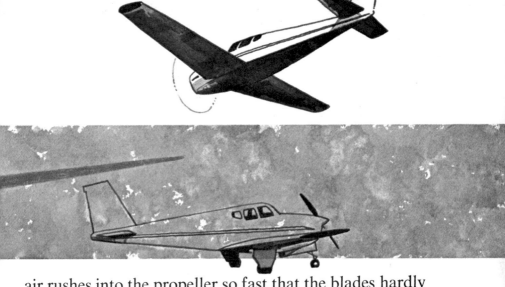

air rushes into the propeller so fast that the blades hardly have time to throw it backward. The faster a plane moves through the air, the less thrust it produces. A propeller produces the most thrust when the plane is standing still!

And Then Came the Jets

In order to fly faster, a new way of powering airplanes had to be found. The answer was provided in 1941 when a young Royal Air Force captain, Frank Whittle, introduced the age of jet flight. Captain Whittle's turbojet engine thrust the first jet airplane through the skies by using the reaction force of a jet.

Whenever a gas or liquid is forced through a nozzle it produces a reaction force in the opposite direction from the jet. It takes several strong firemen to hold a fire hose. They are pushed back by the strong reaction force of the water jet. When a balloon is blown up and released, it

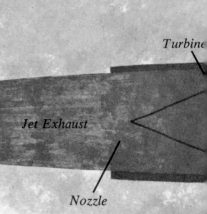

darts rapidly about in the air. The escaping air produces a reaction force on the balloon which thrusts it through the air. When all the air has escaped there is no reaction force and the balloon falls.

Turbine

Jet Exhaust

Nozzle

Fuel T.

The turbojet engine produces a high-speed jet by using the chemical energy in fuel. There are four main parts to a turbojet engine. Air is drawn into the engine by a giant fan called a compressor. The compressor not only sucks in air, but also squeezes it down, thus raising its pressure. It has rows of fixed and moving blades somewhat like a steam turbine.

The pushing air leaves the compressor and enters a combustion chamber. Fuel is sprayed in and the mixture is burned. The chemical energy of the fuel adds to the pressure energy of the air. Once started, the burning in the combustion chamber goes on steadily. But keeping the fire burning in a turbojet is like trying to burn a match in a windstorm!

The next major part of the turbojet is the familiar turbine. The hot pushing gases are speeded up by nozzles

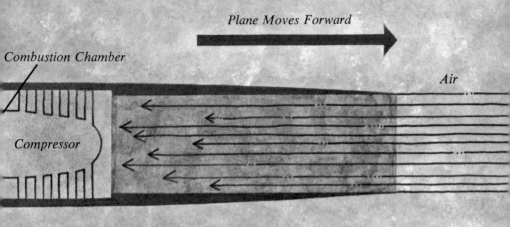

Plane Moves Forward

Combustion Chamber

Air

Compressor

Air is drawn into the engine by the spinning compressor. Here it is compressed, squeezed together. The compressed air enters the combustion chamber where it combines with fuel and burns. The hot gases caused by the burning then turn the turbine, which in turn keeps the compressor spinning. These same hot gases are forced out through the nozzle, causing a terrific reaction force which moves the plane forward.

to whirl the blades of the turbine. The turbine and compressor are attached to the same shaft. Therefore when the turbine turns, the compressor also turns. The energy of the hot gas which drives the turbine is really used to turn the compressor. As long as the compressor and turbine turn, more air will be drawn into the engine.

The real trick however is that only a small part of the energy of the gas is used to drive the turbine. Just behind the turbine is a large jet exhaust nozzle. After passing through the turbine, the hot gases are squeezed down through the small hole in the nozzle. Pushed by new gas from the turbine, the gases speed up through the nozzle to as much as two thousand miles per hour. It is

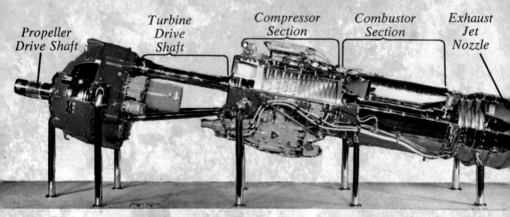

Propeller
Drive Shaft

Turbine
Drive
Shaft

Compressor
Section

Combustor
Section

Exhaust
Jet
Nozzle

In most turboprop engines 80 per cent of the thrust comes from the propeller and about 20 per cent from the exhaust jet.

the giant reaction force from this roaring jet which thrusts the airplane forward.

It is important to remember that the turbojet is an air-breathing engine. A small turbojet engine which produces 3,500 pounds of thrust gulps and throws backward one hundred tons of air in an hour. Anything which forces more air through the engine will increase the thrust. Faster flight speeds ram more air into the engine. This is why the turbojet engine works best at high speeds.

A turbojet becomes a turboprop by extending the shaft enough to attach a propeller. The whirling turbine then drives both the compressor and the propeller. The turbine takes more energy from the hot gases because it turns a propeller in addition to the compressor. However there is still enough energy left in the gas to produce a jet.

54

Rockets—The Oldest and the Newest

One of the oldest and yet the newest of the heat engines is the rocket. Rockets were built and flown for fun by the Chinese almost six hundred years ago. Both rockets and turbojets develop thrust from the reaction force of a high-speed jet. It is only recently however that engineers have been able to build rockets large enough to power missiles and airplanes.

Rocket engines are the most powerful heat engines yet invented. An engine no greater than a barrel can produce 150,000 pounds of thrust. The rocket is a true internal combustion engine, but with one big difference. It is not an air-breathing engine! In all of the other heat engines, the fuel is burned by the oxygen in air. The rocket engine is different. It carries its own oxygen right along with it!

An American, Dr. R. H. Goddard, fired the first liquid fuel rocket in 1926. His rocket, although very small, was much like the giant rockets of today. It used gasoline as a fuel and mixed it with pure oxygen to burn. The oxygen was carried in a separate tank and kept so cold that it was liquid, not gas.

Goddard's Rocket

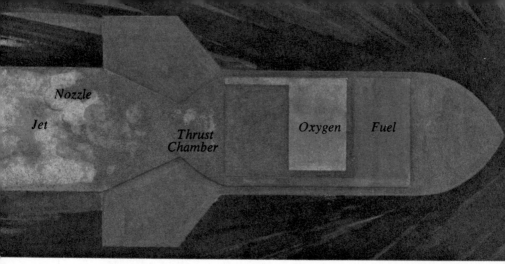

Nozzle

Jet

Thrust
Chamber

Oxygen

Fuel

In a liquid-fuel rocket engine the fuel and oxygen are mixed and burn in the thrust chamber. The burned gas, under great pressure, can then escape only through the jet nozzle.

The heart of the rocket engine is the thrust chamber. The thrust chamber has a specially shaped exhaust nozzle on one end. The fuel and oxygen are kept in separate tanks because of their great explosive energy. They are pumped through separate pipes to the thrust chamber. At the front end of the thrust chamber they are sprayed in through a great many small holes. This mixes them just as a carburetor mixes gasoline and air.

Once ignited they burn steadily and furiously. The burned gas is very hot and under great pressure. It can escape only through the jet nozzle at the end of the thrust chamber. It is the unusual shape of this nozzle which makes the gases rush out at four thousand miles per hour. The chemical energy in the fuel and oxygen forms a red-hot jet traveling faster than the speed of sound!

At a glance the rocket engine seems very simple. It has no pistons or turbine wheels. In fact it has no moving parts at all. The raging combustion however produces temperatures greater than three times the melting point of steel. Like any heat engine, the rocket must be cooled. Sometimes this is done with either the fuel or the oxygen before it enters the engine.

Another type of rocket engine uses solid fuel. Here the fuel and oxidizer are mixed together in the factory to form a solid stick. This is placed in the thrust chamber. Once ignited it burns rapidly on one end. Solid rockets do not need tanks. They carry all of their chemical energy right in the thrust chamber.

It is important to remember that the rocket thrust comes from the reaction force of the high-speed exhaust jet on the thrust chamber. It is not, as some people still believe, the push of the exhaust gas against the outside air which causes the rocket to move. In fact a rocket goes even faster if there is no outside air at all.

If this rocket were closed on all sides, the outward push of the burning fuel would be balanced. One side is open, the push is unbalanced—and the rocket is thrust forward.

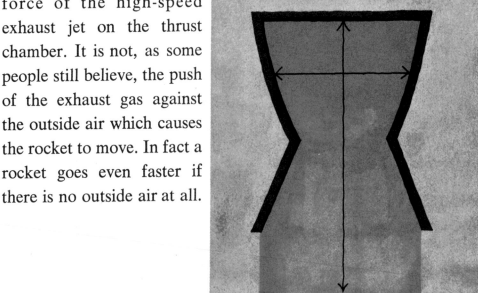

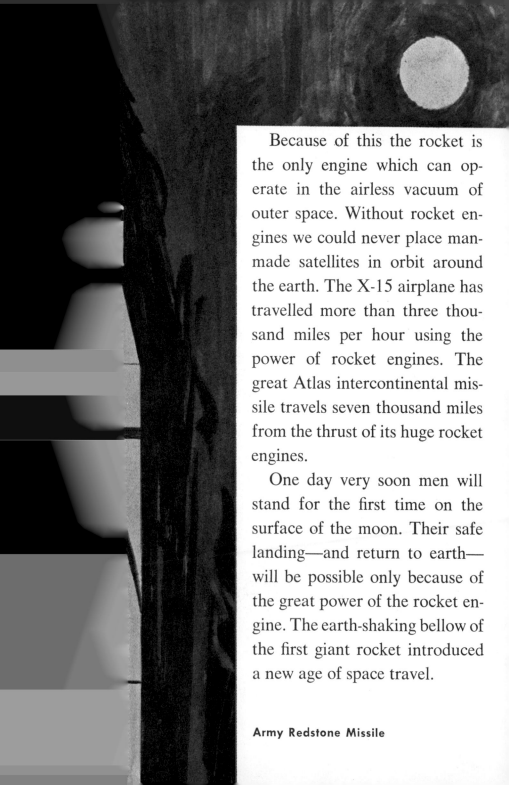

Because of this the rocket is the only engine which can operate in the airless vacuum of outer space. Without rocket engines we could never place man-made satellites in orbit around the earth. The X-15 airplane has travelled more than three thousand miles per hour using the power of rocket engines. The great Atlas intercontinental missile travels seven thousand miles from the thrust of its huge rocket engines.

One day very soon men will stand for the first time on the surface of the moon. Their safe landing—and return to earth—will be possible only because of the great power of the rocket engine. The earth-shaking bellow of the first giant rocket introduced a new age of space travel.

Army Redstone Missile

. . . that to burn one pound of gasoline, air equaling that in an average one-story house must be added to it.

. . . that the peak output of Boulder Dam is one and three-quarter million horsepower. If the Dam operated at this level continuously for three weeks it would produce the same amount of energy that 100,000 slaves expended in the twenty years it took them to build the Pyramid of Cheops.

. . . that an automobile moving at sixty miles per hour travels the length of a football field in about three and one-half seconds. In this short time enough air to fill five household refrigerators passes through the engine. The space occupied by the hot exhaust gas would be equal in size to sixteen refrigerators sitting on the field.

. . . that when a six-cylinder engine moves at high speed, each piston moves up and down a total of one-third mile for each mile the car travels.

. . . that the giant Atlas Missile has three rocket engines which thrust it from its launching pad with a force of 370,000 pounds. Its roaring engines consume one-half ton of liquid oxygen and one-quarter ton of jet fuel every second. If this fuel and oxidizer were contained in tanks the size of an automobile gas tank, the Atlas would empty nineteen tanks for every second that it operated.

59

WHAT IS MOON MILK?

HOW DO ENGINES WORK?

HOW DEEP CAN DIVERS GO?

Whitman
Learn About Books

Lots of full-color pictures and on-the-spot photographs

Loaded with fun-to-know facts

Printed in easy-to-read type

Good sturdy bindings

11 TURN TO THE SEA *by Dr. Athelstan Spilhaus*

Learn how men of the past studied the sea, and how men of the present go down into it. Find out about the sea's strange creatures, about underwater mountains and rivers, and how one day we may farm and mine the sea.

12 CAVES AND THEIR MYSTERIES *by James McClurg*

Caves can be "live" or "dead" and can "breathe" in and out. Find out how caves form, and about soda straws, moon milk, and cave "decorations." And find out who explores caves.

13 ENGINES, PROGRESS AND POWER *by Don E. Rogers*

The first engine was a human engine, man. Learn how man found out how to make animals and water and steam work for him. Find out how gasoline engines, diesel engines, and rocket engines work.

14 YOUR BODY *by Harry Swartz, M.D.*

Learn about yourself. Find out about the cells, tissues, and organs that make up your body . . . about how bone grows and can rebuild itself when it breaks . . . and about the glands that control the workings of your body.

Whitman Learn About Books—carefully prepared with the editorial assistance of specialists in many fields.

Whitman
REG. U.S. PAT. OFF.

BOOKS IN THE LEARN ABOUT SERIES